Introducing
STRAVINSKY

ROLAND VERNON

❦ *Belitha Press*

First published in the UK in 1997 by

Belitha Press Limited,
London House, Great Eastern Wharf,
Parkgate Road, London SW11 4NQ

ISBN 1 85561 545 2

British Library Cataloguing in Publication Data
for this book is available from the British Library.

Printed in Hong Kong

Editors: Christine Hatt and Claire Edwards
Designer: Wilson Design Associates
Picture researcher: Diana Morris

Picture acknowledgements:
AKG, London: front cover background, 9t; 13t © ADAGP Paris &
DACS London; 13b, 14t, 16b, 19b. Bridgeman Art Library: front
cover Haags Gemeentemuseum; 6b Private Collection; 11t British
Library; 14b Musée de l'Opera, Paris © SPADEM, Paris & DACS,
London; 15t Private Collection; 18 Novosti; 21t Giraudon/Musée
Picasso, Paris © Sucession Picasso, Paris & DACS, London; 26t
Sir John Soane Museum, London; 28b Haags Gemeentemuseum.
Camera Press: 28t. Dee Conway: 9b. Corbis-Bettmann: 10t, 11b,
17, 19t, 24t, 25t, 26b, 29t, 29b. E.T. Archive: back cover b, 15b,
18l Musée Quai D'Orsay, © SPADEM, Paris & DACS London;
25b. Mary Evans Picture Library: 10b, 16t, 20; 21tr Explorer.
Hulton Getty Picture Collection: 8b, 22b, 27t. Performing
Arts Library: title page © Louis Ingi; 27b © Clive Barda. Roger-
Viollet/Lipnitzki: 23b, 24b. Collection Theodore Stravinsky:
b cover t, 6t, 7b, 8t, 12t. Reg Wilson: 23t. Zefa: 22t.

CONTENTS

INTRODUCING STRAVINSKY

The beginning of the twentieth century marked a turning point in science and art. Cars and aeroplanes were invented, fresh theories of physics were discovered and terrible new machines of warfare were designed. Painters and musicians rejected nineteenth-century ideas and began to find revolutionary new ways of expressing themselves. Igor Stravinsky grew up in this changing world. From an early age he helped to create modern music. He went on to influence other composers in exciting new ways for more than 50 years. The world continued to change throughout his long and varied life, but Stravinsky was always at the forefront of modern music. His brilliant, precise mind never grew tired of exploring and working out fresh ways to compose. He is generally considered to be the greatest composer of the twentieth century.

A LONELY CHILD

Igor Stravinsky was born on 17 June 1882 at Oranienbaum, a Russian seaside village. His parents were spending the summer holidays there. Soon after his birth, the family travelled back home to the nearby city of St Petersburg, where Igor's father, Fyodor Stravinsky, was a successful **opera** singer. Fyodor was well-known in Russia, not only for his fine voice, but also for his brilliant acting.

Igor had a rather lonely, unhappy childhood. His mother, Anna, was not very affectionate, and Fyodor was a strict father with a violent temper. Igor's two older brothers, Roman and Yuri, were too busy to take an interest in him, and his only real friend at home was his youngest brother, called Guri. The two boys had one special interest in common – music.

Fyodor and Anna Stravinsky. Igor said about his father: 'the only tenderness he ever showed me was when I was ill.'

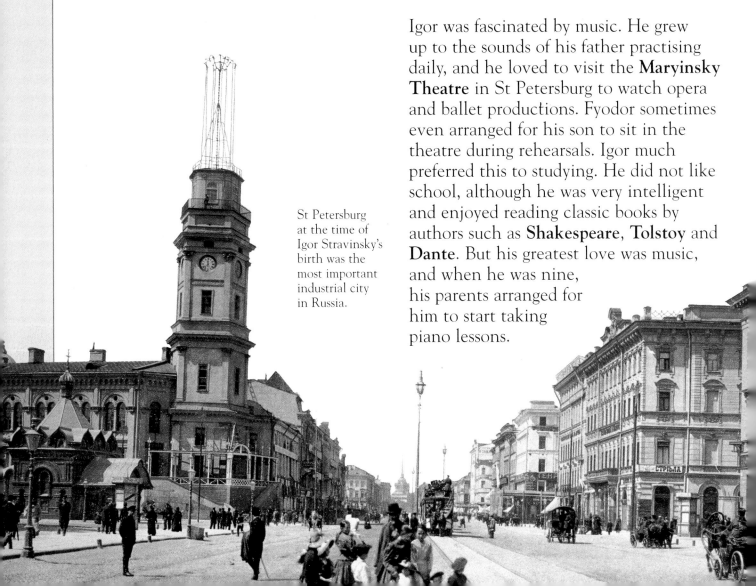

St Petersburg at the time of Igor Stravinsky's birth was the most important industrial city in Russia.

Igor was fascinated by music. He grew up to the sounds of his father practising daily, and he loved to visit the **Maryinsky Theatre** in St Petersburg to watch opera and ballet productions. Fyodor sometimes even arranged for his son to sit in the theatre during rehearsals. Igor much preferred this to studying. He did not like school, although he was very intelligent and enjoyed reading classic books by authors such as **Shakespeare**, **Tolstoy** and **Dante**. But his greatest love was music, and when he was nine, his parents arranged for him to start taking piano lessons.

The young Igor was inspired by the folk music he heard during summer holidays in the Russian countryside.

The Stravinsky family left St Petersburg every summer to stay with relatives in the country. Igor particularly enjoyed hearing folk music and watching the colourful dancing at countryside fairs. His favourite relative in the country was an uncle called Alexander Ielachich. They spent many happy days together, talking about music and playing piano duet versions of music by the great composers of the nineteenth century.

It was on another of these summer visits to the countryside that Igor met his first cousin, Catherine Nossenko. She, too, greatly enjoyed music, and immediately became his best friend. Throughout Igor's childhood, Catherine was like a sister to him.

Igor Stravinsky (right) aged nine, with his younger brother Guri. Guri had a fine voice like his father's.

A PASSION FOR LEARNING

Stravinsky at the age of 18 had a passion for music, but was forced to train for a different career – the law.

*I*gor could soon **sight-read** well on the piano, and began to **improvise** musical ideas of his own. But he was told to stop wasting time, and to concentrate on perfecting his playing. Anna and Fyodor still took little interest in their son's talent for music. But he was given the key to Fyodor's library, which meant that he could spend hours studying his father's huge collection of opera scores. Igor had a passion for learning about music, especially Russian music. Russia had its own musical tradition, and Igor looked back to the great Russian composers of the nineteenth century – Glinka, **Mussorgsky**, **Glazounov**, **Borodin** and Tchaikovsky – for inspiration.

But Igor was also ready to learn more. When a friend introduced him to works by French composers, he began to realize that there was an exciting world of music beyond his Russian homeland.

The University of St Petersburg stood on the River Neva. The city was the capital of Russia from 1712 to 1918.

TCHAIKOVSKY AND RUSSIAN NATIONAL MUSIC

As a boy, Stravinsky once caught sight of Russia's best-known composer at the theatre in St Petersburg. He was Peter Tchaikovsky, and he later became one of Stravinsky's greatest heroes. Tchaikovsky had a genius for drama, and some of his greatest music was written for the theatre. He brought the magnificent tradition of Russian ballet to a high point at the end of the nineteenth century, with works such as *Swan Lake*, *The Sleeping Beauty* and *Nutcracker*. Stravinsky's works for the ballet were strongly affected by Tchaikovsky's achievements.

Tchaikovsky was influenced by a group of Russian composers known as 'The Five', who thought that Russian music should be inspired by Russian life and culture. For example, they used real folk tunes to give their music a genuinely Russian feel. The most determined of these **nationalist** composers was Mily Balakirev (1837–1910). His ideas originated in the work of Mikhail Glinka (1804–1857), who was known as the father of Russian music. It was this national style that Stravinsky inherited.

Peter Tchaikovsky (1840–1893) suffered long bouts of depression in later life.

As soon as he finished school, in 1901, Igor wanted to start a career in music. But his parents persuaded him to train for a job that would provide a good, safe income. He was therefore sent to the University of St Petersburg to study law.

Igor's four years at university were very frustrating. He was not at all interested in law, and preferred to spend time teaching himself to compose. He experimented by arranging other composers' works for the piano. Slowly, he began to write short piano pieces of his own, in the style of the Russian composers he most admired.

On 21 November 1902, Fyodor Stravinsky died. Although Igor was sad to lose his father, he now felt free to make his own decisions. First, he wanted to meet a really good music teacher. He was finally able to do this thanks to a friend he had made at university earlier in 1902 – Vladimir Rimsky-Korsakov.

Vladimir's world-famous father was one of Russia's greatest composers – Nikolai Rimsky-Korsakov. Igor needed the advice of an experienced composer, so he decided to try to meet his friend's father.

A ballerina dancing in Tchaikovsky's *Nutcracker*.

RIMSKY-KORSAKOV

Nikolai Rimsky-Korsakov was a patriotic man who deliberately wrote music that would sound Russian.

Nikolai Rimsky-Korsakov (1844–1908) was a leading member of 'The Five', the most influential group of composers working in Russia at the time. In 1902, Igor was invited to stay with the Rimsky-Korsakov family, who were spending the summer holidays in the German town of Heidelberg. When Igor arrived in Germany, he played some of his piano pieces to the great composer. Rimsky-Korsakov listened carefully and said that the young man should keep up the good work because he still had much to learn. Igor was a little depressed by this, but realized later that it was good advice.

THE RUSSIAN REVOLUTION OF 1905

Towards the end of the nineteenth century, there was much unrest in the Russian empire. Workers, peasants and intellectuals felt that **Tsar** Nicholas II's rule was very harsh. Millions of people lived in miserable poverty. Matters grew worse when Russia started a pointless war with Japan, in 1904, and suffered disastrous defeats.

On 22 January 1905, a huge crowd of workers gathered in front of the Tsar's palace in St Petersburg. The army fired on them and hundreds were killed or injured. This tragic event became known as Bloody Sunday, and it led to strikes and rebellions across the empire. There were also **mutinies** in the army and navy. A general strike was called in October 1905, and people's councils planned to overthrow the government. The Tsar survived only by promising to set up an elected parliament. This satisfied people for the moment, and the strikes ended. In many parts of the empire, troops had to use violence to stamp out the last of the revolution.

A revolutionary crowd in St Petersburg in 1905.

Back in St Petersburg, Igor regularly visited Rimsky-Korsakov's house. There he met other ambitious young musicians, and exchanged ideas. He also made friends with an interesting group of artists and intellectuals. They organized 'Evenings of **Contemporary** Music', to try out new music, not just from Russia, but from all over Europe. In this way, Stravinsky began to develop his musical ideas.

Claude Debussy (1862–1918) was a revolutionary composer and a brilliant pianist. He later got to know Stravinsky very well and greatly admired his work.

Of all the new composers he heard, Igor was most fascinated by the work of a Frenchman, Claude Debussy. He composed in a strange and beautiful new language, in which effects and atmosphere were more important than tunes.

Life in St Petersburg was very tense at this time, because of a revolution that had taken place in 1905. There were soldiers everywhere, and a feeling that at any moment violence might break out. Igor was not very interested in politics unless it interfered with his career. Later in life, he moved and even changed nationality to find a peaceful atmosphere for work.

Igor now became Rimsky-Korsakov's pupil. Rimsky taught him what each type of instrument in an orchestra was capable of playing. He also explained how to compose for an orchestra so that the different groups of instruments would sound properly balanced. Igor listened to all this helpful advice. As a result, some of his early compositions sounded very much like works by Rimsky-Korsakov himself!

Tsar Nicholas II of Russia (left) and King George V of England were first cousins. They were both grandsons of England's Queen Victoria.

DEATH OF A FRIEND

I. gor finished his studies at the University of St Petersburg in 1905, and shortly afterwards married his cousin Catherine. He completed his first major composition for orchestra, the **Symphony** in E flat, in 1907. It was an old-fashioned work, and showed little of his growing interest in modern French music. Rimsky-Korsakov and the older Russian composers disliked modern music. They thought that if music broke the basic rules of composition, it was bad music. But Igor was beginning to think that breaking the rules gave music a freedom and freshness it had not had in the past.

Stravinsky was devoted to his wife and childhood friend, Catherine. After her death he married again, but he always spoke fondly of Catherine in later life.

The meeting of Diaghilev and Stravinsky in 1909 was an historic event. As a result of their friendship, music was never the same again.

Russian artist Wassily Kandinsky (1866–1944) was inventing this new style of painting as Stravinsky was experimenting with revolutionary new forms of music.

Serge Diaghilev (1872–1929) was not particularly talented in any of the arts, but he had a huge knowledge of painting, dance and music.

Rimsky-Korsakov's daughter, Nadezhda, planned to get married in 1908. To celebrate the event, Igor wrote an orchestral piece called *Fireworks*. When the work was complete, he posted it to his teacher for approval. But the package was returned shortly afterwards, with a message saying that Rimsky-Korsakov had died. Igor was deeply upset, and left at once for the funeral. *Fireworks* was eventually performed in February 1909, and it showed that Igor was beginning to create his own style. Now he was ready to break with tradition.

Serge Diaghilev, a leading figure in the artistic life of Russia, was listening to *Fireworks* that night. Diaghilev promoted new art and modern music. He organized grand exhibitions, concerts, operas and ballets in order to bring Western European art to Russia, and take Russian art to the West. He had a powerful personality and was clever at spotting talent. In 1906, he put on an exhibition of Russian paintings and several concerts of Russian music in Paris. He was enormously successful, and soon became one of the most fashionable people in the city.

Just at the time Diaghilev heard Stravinsky's *Fireworks*, he was gathering together a ballet company to visit Paris. He had found the best Russian dancers and the most imaginative designers. All he needed now was a composer of exciting new music.

A TURNING POINT

Diaghilev wanted a new ballet for his company to perform in Paris, as part of the 1910 **season**. He invited Stravinsky to compose it for him. The story Diaghilev had chosen for the work was a Russian fairy tale, *The Firebird*. It was about a prince who falls in love with a princess and rescues her with the help of a magic bird. Igor finished it in six months, just in time for the rehearsals.

From the start, everyone who heard *The Firebird* was amazed. It used a huge orchestra, which meant that the overall sound was rich and magnificent. In many ways it was like the work of Nikolai Rimsky-Korsakov, especially its style of using different groups of instruments for special effects. But *The Firebird* was also influenced by modern music. It contained complicated, violent rhythms that old-fashioned people found very shocking.

The greatest male dancer in Diaghilev's Ballets Russes was Vaslav Nijinsky. He is seen here in costume for Rimsky-Korsakov's ballet *Scheherazade*.

Tamara Karsavina, one of the star ballerinas in the Ballets Russes. Here, she is performing the leading role of the magic Firebird in Stravinsky's great ballet.

The first performance of *The Firebird*, on 25 June 1910, was a triumph. Stravinsky became a star overnight. Suddenly, everyone in Paris wanted to meet him – famous composers, artists and writers, even Debussy, whom Igor had so long admired.

The following autumn, Stravinsky began composing a concert piece for orchestra and piano. Diaghilev asked him to turn it into a new ballet for the next Paris season. Stravinsky chose the story this time. It was about a puppet character called Petrushka, who magically comes to life. The music for *Petrushka* was even more daring than the inventive score of *The Firebird*.

Diaghilev's Ballets Russes

Serge Diaghilev knew that Russia had the finest ballet dancers in the world, but he also realized that the old-fashioned style of dancing, known as **classical ballet**, had become stale and uninteresting. He wanted to take Russian dancers to theatres in Western Europe, and therefore decided that a new style of ballet would have to be invented. His plan was to bring together imaginative scenery and costumes with interesting new dance steps and fresh music. He called his company the Ballets Russes (Russian Ballet). Stravinsky's brilliant new music became a vital part of the Ballets Russes' amazing success.

Diaghilev's dancers included the extraordinary Vaslav Nijinsky (1890–1950), whose athletic leaps and unusual movements both shocked and thrilled audiences. Tragically, Nijinsky's career was cut short by insanity. Diaghilev also employed adventurous designers such as Leon Bakst (1866–1924), and imaginative choreographers such as Michel Fokine (1880–1942). Between 1909 and Diaghilev's death in 1929, the Ballets Russes was one of Europe's most daring and important artistic groups.

A design by Leon Bakst for Rimsky-Korsakov's *Scheherazade*.

A painting of Nijinsky dancing the role of the puppet Petrushka. It is one of the most difficult roles for a dancer to perform.

Stravinsky was now an independent composer with his own style. One of the most important new ideas he used in *Petrushka* was called polytonality. This means music written in two different **keys** but played at the same time. Stravinsky's polytonality added a powerful, clashing effect to his music, and many other composers soon began to imitate it.

Petrushka was Stravinsky's second huge success. The Russian dancers, especially Nijinsky, performed superbly. The costumes, **set designs** and **choreography** were stunning. Stravinsky, still only 29 years old, was now established as one of the most exciting composers in the world.

Stravinsky's ballets were attended by some of the richest people in Paris. In this picture, the audience arrives at a Paris theatre for an evening of grand musical entertainment.

A MUSICAL EARTHQUAKE

Stravinsky's next ballet was so unusual that it shook the world of music like an earthquake. The idea for the story came in a daydream. He imagined a **pagan** religious ceremony, in which a young girl dances herself to death to honour the god of spring.

Diaghilev immediately wanted the new work for the Ballets Russes. It was chosen for the 1913 season in Paris, and called *The Rite of Spring*. Vaslav Nijinsky was to be the choreographer. During the rehearsals, Stravinsky was very active, helping Nijinsky and the ballet dancers to understand his complicated new music.

Stravinsky's handwritten manuscript for *The Rite of Spring*. Stravinsky's musical handwriting was well-known for its extreme neatness.

The first night, on 29 May 1913, was a disaster. From the first notes, the audience began to laugh. This turned into booing, whistling and shouting. The uproar was so loud that the dancers could not even hear the orchestra. Stravinsky walked out in a fury, while Diaghilev tried to calm everyone down.

People were so upset because they were used to easy tunes and pleasant **harmonies**, but *The Rite of Spring* had neither. It was fierce, savage music, full of pounding rhythms and **dissonant** sounds. Stravinsky's enemies said that he deliberately wrote ugly music simply so that he could call himself revolutionary. But others thought that the work was a masterpiece. Many young composers imitated *The Rite of Spring*. It had established Stravinsky as a hero of modern music.

THE FIRST WORLD WAR

At the beginning of the twentieth century, the richest countries of Europe rivalled each other for power, both at home and in **colonies** abroad. There was a massive build-up of weapons. Eventually, the countries split into two groups, and war broke out across Europe in summer 1914. Russia, France, Great Britain and Italy (the Allies) fought against Germany, Austria-Hungary and Turkey. Japan and the United States later joined in on the side of the Allies. About 10 million people were killed before the war ended in 1918.

The First World War was the first conflict in which modern fighting equipment and techniques were used, such as tanks, machine guns, poison gas, aeroplanes and submarines. No one was prepared for the terrible effects, and millions died. Russia was particularly badly affected by the war. Many starved, and people lost trust in the Tsar and his government. There were street riots and mutinies in the army.

This scene from the First World War shows a solitary Russian soldier looking out from a trench.

Immediately after *The Rite of Spring*'s first performance, Stravinsky fell seriously ill with **typhoid**. After recovering, he worked on an opera, *The Nightingale*, and Serge Diaghilev organized the production. Although the opera was appreciated, it did not interest people anything like as much as the three earlier ballets.

However, by now political events were stirring that would completely change not only Stravinsky's life, but those of millions of other people for ever. The horror of the First World War was about to begin.

Stravinsky stormed out of *The Rite of Spring*'s first performance when the whole audience began to jeer and laugh at this revolutionary ballet.

By the age of 30, Stravinsky was famous across the world for his adventurous new style of composing.

A COMPOSER IN EXILE

While the war raged in Europe, Stravinsky lived peacefully in Switzerland, along with a number of artists and musicians from many countries. He missed Russia very much, and never dreamed that his **exile** would last nearly 50 years. The war meant that almost all Europe's musical events were cancelled. Diaghilev was forced to close down the Ballets Russes, but he did manage to get his dancers back together in 1916, for a tour of the United States.

Vladimir Lenin, leader of the Russian Revolution, gives a rousing speech to a crowd of workers in 1917.

During this difficult time, there was little chance of any new **commissions**, so Stravinsky began to run short of money. He was cut off from Russia, his property, his publishers and his **royalties**. He now had four children to support, so it was vital to find some work. 1917 was a depressing year. News reached Stravinsky from Russia that his beloved brother, Guri, had died of **typhus**. Then, in November, came the Russian Revolution. Russians in exile realized that this meant they would probably lose their property at home.

THE RISE OF COMMUNISM IN RUSSIA

The First World War proved to be disastrous for the Russian empire. By 1917, public feeling against Tsar Nicholas II was even stronger than it had been in 1905. He was forced to **abdicate**, and Russia was ruled by a temporary government. In November 1917, another revolution brought a **communist** politician called Vladimir Lenin to power. Lenin took Russia out of the war and gave land to the peasants. The Tsar and his family were executed, and the empire was renamed the Soviet Union.

By the 1920s, communist rule had turned into a **dictatorship**. After Lenin's death, in 1924, Josef Stalin rose to power, and ruled until 1953. He created a **police state** in which people lost almost all their freedom. Those who opposed him risked being murdered. Stalin considered the United States and Western Europe to be enemies of communism. Hundreds of thousands of educated Russians, like Stravinsky, lived abroad to escape the hardship of communist rule. The Soviet government called them traitors and they were not welcome to return.

Stravinsky now had to come up with an idea for something that could be performed in spite of the war in Europe. Together with a close friend, the Swiss writer CF Ramuz, he wrote a small-scale musical work for the stage.

The ruthless Soviet dictator Josef Stalin (right), shown here in 1931.

The Tsar with his son after the Revolution (left). They were later imprisoned and executed.

This new work, *The Soldier's Tale*, involved actors, dancers and instrumentalists. In it, Stravinsky once and for all broke away from the grand Russian style of music. There was no huge orchestra, no lush sound. He stripped his music down to the basics, and used only seven instruments to give it a cleaner sound. The composer was moving towards a completely new style.

The work had a highly successful first performance, on 28 September 1918. But all plans to take it on a tour of Switzerland were cancelled when an epidemic of **Spanish influenza** broke out and Stravinsky caught it.

A NEW DIRECTION

After the war, Stravinsky began to feel restless in Switzerland, and in 1920 he travelled to Paris. It was the artistic capital of the world, a city full of brilliant young artists, writers and musicians. Stravinsky soon became part of their group. In 1934 he became a French citizen and remained in France until 1939.

The end of the war allowed Diaghilev to rebuild his company and plan a new partnership with Stravinsky. In 1922 he put on the composer's new opera, *Mavra*. It was a complete failure. The audience was expecting something big and stirring, like the great ballets before the war. But Stravinsky was no longer interested in writing large-scale, powerful music. He now used a new style, **neo-classicism**.

Stravinsky first became interested in music from the **classical** era in 1920. He was adapting music by the Italian composer Giovanni Battista Pergolesi (1710–1736) for a ballet called *Pulcinella*. Stravinsky fell in love with the style and structure of Pergolesi's eighteenth-century music. From that moment on, his own music was very much influenced by the music of the past, especially works by Bach and **Mozart**.

The German composer Johann Sebastian Bach (1685–1750), who influenced Stravinsky.

Stravinsky's new music was still modern, with spiky rhythms and dissonant notes. But now it followed many of the classical rules. Early examples of his neo-classical works include the **Octet**, of 1923, and the *Piano* **Concerto**, 1924. Audiences found this music harder to understand. It was very clever and neat, but not so exciting. Intellectuals still admired Stravinsky, but he was never as popular with the public as he had been before the First World War.

In order to make some money, Stravinsky decided in 1924 to start performing his own works around the world, either as a conductor or a pianist. The public were especially interested to see him conduct earlier works, such as *The Firebird*. Later in life, the composer claimed to have conducted this piece over 1,000 times.

Stravinsky and his family were happy in Paris. There were many other Russians living there who had escaped from the communist dictatorship in their homeland.

PABLO PICASSO (1881–1973)

During the First World War, Stravinsky made friends with Pablo Picasso, who is considered by many to be the greatest painter of the twentieth century. Born in Spain, Picasso spent most of his life in France. His paintings are often compared to Stravinsky's music. Both men were pioneers who invented new styles as their art developed.

Picasso did not think painting should show the world realistically, like a photograph. He believed that mood and feeling could be expressed in new ways. To begin with, he did this by using certain colours, most often blues or pinks. Then, he changed the shapes of objects. Like Stravinsky, Picasso was inspired by classical art. Some of his figures are based on ancient Greek sculptures.

Picasso also designed theatre sets for Diaghilev, and worked with Stravinsky on the ballet *Pulcinella*. Like Stravinsky, he lived to a great age, and experimented with new forms of art until the end.

An example of one of Picasso's neo-classical paintings. The woman's body, her dreamy expression, her hairstyle and even her dress are based on ancient Greek sculptures.

Inspired by the Ancient World

Stravinsky now began to think of writing a completely different kind of work for the stage. He greatly admired ancient Greek literature, so he decided that his next theatre work would be based on a drama from ancient Greece.

The dramatic ceremonies and music of the Russian Orthodox Church were a great inspiration to Stravinsky.

Jean Cocteau (1889–1963) wrote the words to Stravinsky's *Oedipus Rex*. He was a gifted artist, writer and film director.

The drama Stravinsky chose was *Oedipus Rex*, a play by **Sophocles**. It was about a young man who kills his own father and marries his mother without recognizing either of them. The French playwright Jean Cocteau agreed to write the words, and the work was first performed in May 1927.

Oedipus Rex is one of Stravinsky's greatest neo-classical works. It is a mixture of opera and concert, in which the singers perform in costume, but do not act. The words are in Latin, which gives it an ancient and sacred feel. It sounds almost like religious music. Stravinsky was developing a strong interest in religion at this time, and all his new music began to reveal this.

One important work in which Stravinsky openly expressed his Christian faith was the *Symphony of Psalms*, written for full-scale orchestra and chorus in 1930. Like *Oedipus Rex*, the *Symphony of Psalms* is carefully structured and written in Latin.

Serge Diaghilev and Stravinsky were gradually growing apart. This was partly because Diaghilev was jealous whenever Stravinsky wrote music for companies other than the Ballets Russes. Tragically, Diaghilev died in August 1929. Despite their recent quarrel, Stravinsky felt that he had lost a very dear friend and colleague.

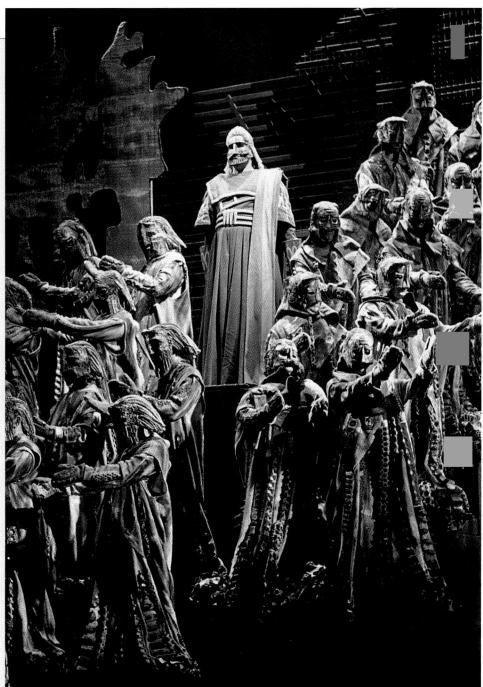

The characters in this 1972 production of *Oedipus Rex* (above) wear masks, in the style of ancient Greek dramas.

Stravinsky's son, Soulima (left), in 1933. Soulima inherited his father's talent for music and the two men often worked together.

Soon after his death, Diaghilev's company, the Ballets Russes, collapsed. But by this time, Stravinsky was composing for a new company. It was run by one of Diaghilev's former ballerinas, Ida Rubinstein.

Apart from his stage works, Stravinsky continued to write piano music to perform on his tours. He also composed for his son, Soulima, who was becoming a fine pianist. The *Concerto for Two Solo Pianos* was completed in 1935 especially so that father and son could perform it together.

Adolf Hitler (centre) built up Germany's army in the 1930s and prepared to invade several neighbouring countries.

NEW LIFE IN THE UNITED STATES

November 1938 to June 1939 was one of the darkest periods in Stravinsky's life. His daughter Ludmilla and his wife Catherine died of **tuberculosis**. His mother also died soon after. The future, too, looked depressing, as the rise of **Adolf Hitler** in Germany brought Europe to the brink of war again.

At this time, Stravinsky was invited to give a course of lectures at Harvard University, in the United States. He left France in September 1939, just at the start of the Second World War. Europe now had little to offer him. He needed peace to compose, and felt that his music was appreciated much more in the United States than in Europe.

Once the lectures were over, Stravinsky started a new life in the United States. In 1940, he married his friend Vera de Bosset, and settled down in **Hollywood**, California. Hollywood was home to many artists, writers and musicians who had fled the war in Europe. Some of Stravinsky's friends were there, and some rivals, such as Austrian composer Arnold Schoenberg.

Vera de Bosset was an actress and a talented artist who became Igor Stravinsky's close friend as early as 1921.

ARNOLD SCHOENBERG AND SERIALISM

The other great pioneer of modern music in the early part of the twentieth century was the Austrian composer Arnold Schoenberg (1874–1951). Schoenberg began his career under the influence of the great nineteenth-century German composers, such as **Wagner** and **Mahler**. But then he rejected the traditional rules of harmony and melody. His new music was described as atonal, which meant that it did not use key signatures and was largely dissonant. Later, Schoenberg developed a new system of composing, called 'twelve-tone music' or 'serialism'. This used a scale of twelve notes – like a normal scale on a piano, but including all the black notes as well as the white notes. These notes were collected into special rows, which formed the basic building-blocks of a serialist composition.

Schoenberg arrived in the United States in 1933 and stayed there for the rest of his life.

Until about 1950, Stravinsky and Schoenberg composed completely different types of modern music. Neither of them liked the other. But Stravinsky changed during the last 20 years of his life, and began to write serial music of his own.

During his first few years in Hollywood, Stravinsky received many requests to write film music, most of which he turned down. But he did compose a ballet for the circus, called *Circus Polka*. It was written to be performed by a troupe of elephants wearing tutus!

At this time, Stravinsky also completed some new works for **symphony orchestra**. The *Symphony in Three* **Movements** was composed to celebrate the end of the Second World War. Parts of it describe the ugliness of war, and sound like his earlier compositions. Audiences thrilled to hear passages that reminded them of *The Rite of Spring*.

Stravinsky loved his exciting new life in the United States. He liked the special treatment that he received there because of his fame, and also particularly enjoyed the warm Californian weather. In 1945, the composer became an American citizen. He continued to live in the United States for the rest of his life.

On 7 December 1941, Japanese planes bombed American ships at Pearl Harbor, Hawaii and the Americans entered the Second World War.

William Hogarth did drawings and paintings of *The Rake's Progress*. This is one of the scenes from the series painted in 1733.

ANOTHER CHANGE OF STYLE

WH Auden (1907–1973) was English by birth, but travelled to the United States in 1939, where he became an American citizen.

After his huge symphony, Stravinsky wrote a small **jazz** concerto for **clarinettist** Woody Herman. The *Ebony Concerto* showed that Stravinsky still enjoyed trying exciting new musical ideas. It had the structure of an eighteenth-century work, but included jazz rhythms and harmonies.

In 1947, the composer saw a set of drawings by **William Hogarth** called *The Rake's Progress*. They told the story of a man who spends all his money, becomes a drunkard and ends up in a mad-house. It is a **moral tale**, but humorous, because the pictures are like cartoons. Stravinsky thought the story was perfect for an opera, and asked the poet WH Auden to write the words. The first performance of *The Rake's Progress* took place in Venice, in September 1951.

Stravinsky talks to his young assistant, Robert Craft. As Stravinsky grew older, Craft began to conduct in his place.

Many people thought that Stravinsky was taking up serialism just so that he could call himself the leader of modern music. They also found some of his serial works rather complicated and difficult to understand. But trained musicians could see that Stravinsky's music showed similarities throughout his life. Serialism just helped him to organize his ideas in a new way.

The Rake's Progress is usually performed in eighteenth-century costumes that have been modernized, like these colourful outfits.

Just as Stravinsky was beginning to write *The Rake's Progress*, he met a young American musician called Robert Craft. They got on well, and Craft was soon employed as the composer's assistant and advisor. Their friendship brought about another complete change of style in Stravinsky's music. Craft persuaded the composer to study serial, or twelve-tone, music. This new technique had been invented by Stravinsky's three main rivals, Arnold Schoenberg, **Alban Berg** and **Anton von Webern**.

Stravinsky's first experiments with the twelve-tone system were cautious, but by 1957 he was composing masterpieces of serial music. The first of these was a large-scale religious work for orchestra and singers, called *Threni*. Stravinsky chose Latin words for the piece, as he had done for his earlier sacred music. They are taken from The Lamentations of Jeremiah, a book in the Old Testament of the Bible that describes the destruction of Jerusalem and its temple.

RETURN TO RUSSIA

Stravinsky is cheered by a Russian audience after nearly 50 years in exile. It was a moving moment for the composer.

Despite his age, Stravinsky kept up a busy schedule travelling and performing abroad. In 1962, he celebrated his 80th birthday, and to mark the occasion, was invited to visit Russia. Although he was very opposed to its communist government, he still thought of Russia as home. So, in September 1962, after an exile of 48 years, Igor Stravinsky returned to the land of his birth. During his visit, he attended many concerts and grand parties. Everywhere he went, he was received like a hero. It was a great and happy experience for the old composer.

Stravinsky was deeply saddened the following year by the **assassination** of the young American president, John F Kennedy, on 22 November 1963. As a mark of respect, he composed a short song known as *Elegy* for JFK, with words by WH Auden. He hoped this work would help people to remember the dead leader.

Stravinsky was devoting more and more time to religious music. In 1966, he completed his last masterpiece, a mass for the dead, called the **Requiem Canticles**. It was for solo singers, chorus and orchestra. While writing it, Stravinsky had a feeling that it might be used at his own funeral.

Stravinsky now began to travel and compose less. He was becoming frail, and his health was unstable. His greatest pleasure was to spend evenings listening to records and discussing them with Robert Craft. In 1969, he moved to New York, so that he could receive better medical help. He died there, aged 88, on 6 April 1971.

Even in old age, Stravinsky continued to take an active part in some performances of his works.

THE ASSASSINATION OF JOHN F KENNEDY

John F Kennedy was the youngest man ever to be president of the United States. He was good-looking, popular and a strong leader. In 1963, he was campaigning around the country to be re-elected as president for a second time. As part of his tour, he visited Dallas, a town in Texas. While driving through the town in an open car, waving to the crowds, he was shot dead.

The man accused of the assassination was Lee Harvey Oswald. However, Oswald was also assassinated before he had the chance to stand trial. There have been many theories about the assassination, some of which say that secret agents and criminal organizations were responsible. But Oswald is still officially named as the killer.

President Kennedy smiles at crowds just moments before his shooting.

Stravinsky's body was flown to Venice, Italy, where a grand funeral was held at the church of San Giovanni e Paolo. The *Requiem Canticles* were sung.

Stravinsky's body was then taken by boat across the Venice lagoon to the island of San Michele, to be buried. Just a few steps away was the grave of his friend Diaghilev.

Stravinsky's coffin, accompanied by a Russian Orthodox priest, is rowed across the lagoon of Venice in a gondola.

TIME CHART

1882	Igor Stravinsky born at Oranienbaum, Russia, 17 June.
1902	Meets Nikolai Rimsky-Korsakov. Fyodor Stravinsky dies, 21 November.
1905	Bloody Sunday, part of the 1905 Russian Revolution, 22 January. Finishes his studies at the University of St Petersburg.
1906	Marries Catherine Nossenko, 24 January.
1908	Death of Rimsky-Korsakov, 21 June.
1909	First performance of *Fireworks*, 6 February. Begins friendship with Serge Diaghilev.
1910	First performance of *The Firebird*, 25 June.
1911	First performance of *Petrushka*, 13 June.
1913	First performance of *The Rite of Spring*, 29 May.
1914	Outbreak of the First World War. Stravinsky moves to Switzerland.
1917	Russian Revolution.
1918	First performance of *The Soldier's Tale*, 28 September. First World War finishes, 11 November.
1920	Moves to Paris.
1922	First performance of *Mavra*, 3 June.
1924	Begins career performing his own works.
1927	First performance of *Oedipus Rex*, 30 May.
1929	Death of Diaghilev, 19 August.
1934	Becomes a French citizen, 10 June.
1938	Stravinsky's daughter, Ludmilla, dies, 30 November.
1939	Stravinsky's wife, Catherine, dies, 2 March. Stravinsky's mother dies, 7 June. Leaves Europe for the United States, September. Second World War begins.
1940	Marries Vera de Bosset, 9 March.
1945	Second World War finishes, 8 May. Becomes American citizen, 28 December.
1948	Meets Robert Craft, 31 March.
1951	First performance of *The Rake's Progress*, 11 September.
1958	First performance of *Threni*, 23 September.
1962	Returns to Russia, 21 September.
1963	John F Kennedy assassinated, Dallas, United States, 22 November.
1966	First performance of *Requiem Canticles*, 8 October.
1971	Igor Stravinsky dies in New York, 6 April.

GLOSSARY

abdicate to resign from a position of power or leadership.

assassination murder (usually of famous people).

Berg, Alban (1885–1935) Austrian composer and pupil of Arnold Schoenberg. Above all, he is respected for his two operas *Wozzeck* and *Lulu*.

Borodin, Alexander (1833–1887) Russian composer and doctor. One of 'The Five' Russian nationalist composers, he wrote only a few works.

canticles short religious verses that can be set to music for singing.

choreography the plan for a ballet, including the steps and movements.

clarinettist a person who plays the clarinet, which is a wind instrument, usually made of black wood.

classical in music, this refers to the period from around 1750 to 1820, a time when people admired the art and literature of ancient Greece and Rome – the classical civilizations. Classical compositions used formal structures, rather than allowing the composer to express his own feelings.

classical ballet a system of ballet dancing based on a strict set of rules, movements and positions. Classical ballet reached its height during the late nineteenth century in Russia.

colony a country that is owned and ruled by another country.

commission an invitation from an employer to a composer to write a piece of music for an agreed price.

communist a person who believes in a political system in which all property is shared equally. The founder of communist ideas was the German writer Karl Marx (1818–1883).

concerto a piece of music written for orchestra and solo instruments.

contemporary a word used to describe things that happen or are being created now, in the present era.

Dante, Alighieri (1265–1321) Italian poet, born in Florence, whose most famous work was *The Divine Comedy*, in which he imagines a journey down to hell and on to paradise.

dictatorship the political situation in a country ruled by one person (a dictator) who has absolute power over everybody else.

dissonant containing musical sounds in which different notes played at the same time clash with one another.

elegy a funeral song, written to mark somebody's death.

exile when people live in a foreign country and cannot return to their homeland, they are described as 'in exile'. They are also called 'exiles'.

Glazounov, Alexander (1865–1936) Russian composer and pupil of Rimsky-Korsakov. After the 1917 Russian Revolution, he was popular with the communist government, but later went to live in Paris.

harmony the way musical notes are arranged so that they fit in with each other neatly.

Hitler, Adolf (1889–1945) German politician who became a dictator. Hitler built up his country's power during the 1930s, and led Germany into the Second World War.

Hogarth, William (1697–1764) English artist who specialized in drawing sets of pictures, each of which tells a story and carries a moral. The pictures are also humorous.

Hollywood a district of California, near Los Angeles, that is particularly famous for being the centre of the United States film industry.

improvise to compose a piece of music, or a new version of a piece of music, while actually performing it.

jazz a type of music that comes originally from the black population of the United States. Jazz was born in the late nineteenth century and became hugely fashionable by the 1920s. It involves a special kind of harmony and distinctive rhythms.

key the 'family' to which a particular piece of music belongs. Music is grouped into 24 families. They are known by letters (A, B, C, D, E, F and G), together with variations ('sharp' and 'flat', 'major' and 'minor').

Mahler, Gustav (1860–1911) Austrian composer and conductor admired for his nine symphonies.

Maryinsky Theatre a grand theatre in the centre of St Petersburg, where many of the greatest Russian works for the stage had their first performances.

moral tale a story that contains a special message of advice, or a warning of what might happen if someone does not behave well.

movement a piece of music that forms part of a larger composition. A typical symphony or concerto is divided into three or four movements.

Mozart, Wolfgang Amadeus (1756–1791) Austrian composer, often described as the most brilliant musical genius in history. Although he only lived a short while, he produced vast numbers of works, most of which are masterpieces.

Mussorgsky, Modest (1835–1881) one of 'The Five' nationalist Russian composers, and a friend of Rimsky-Korsakov. He is best remembered for his opera *Boris Godunov*.

mutiny a revolt in the army or navy, when soldiers rebel against their senior officers.

nationalist strongly in support of one's own country and culture.

neo-classicism a style of modern art or music that is influenced either by the classical period of the eighteenth century, or by the ancient arts of Greece and Rome.

octet a piece of music written for eight instruments or voices.

opera a musical drama in which the performers sing most or all of their lines. The music is just as important as the words in an opera.

pagan a word used to describe a religion, a religious person or a religious ceremony that is not recognized by the Christian, Jewish or Islamic faiths. 'Pagan' usually refers to pre-Christian religions.

police state a country in which unusually strict rules are enforced by the authorities, together with the police and army.

requiem a Christian church ceremony usually performed at funerals.

royalty money earned by a composer or author when his or her work is published or recorded and sold.

season a portion of the year (weeks or months) dedicated to a particular activity, for example concerts, exhibitions or parties.

set design the design for the scenery in a theatre production.

Shakespeare, William (1564–1616) English poet and playwright, admired across the world as one of the greatest writers who ever lived.

sight-read to play music at sight, reading it for the first time from written notes.

Sophocles (about 496–405 BC) Greek playwright who wrote *Oedipus Rex*. Of his 100 works, only seven survive.

Spanish influenza an infectious disease affecting the nose, throat and lungs, which killed many people in the period after the First World War.

symphony a large-scale piece of music usually written for orchestra alone, but in some cases also involving other performers (for example, Stravinsky's work *Symphony of Psalms*, which includes singers).

symphony orchestra an orchestra large enough to play large-scale works.

Tolstoy, Leo (1828–1910) Russian author who also worked to reform politics. He is best known for his long novel *War and Peace*.

Tsar the title given to the kings of Russia.

tuberculosis an infection that attacks the lungs. Before a cure was found, tuberculosis killed many people.

typhoid an infectious disease that attacks the bowels and brings on a high fever.

typhus a disease carried to humans by lice. It is common in times of terrible war and famine.

Wagner, Richard (1813–1883) German composer of opera. Wagner was a headstrong nationalist with a great gift for the stage. He greatly influenced the history of opera.

Webern, Anton von (1883–1945) Austrian composer and pupil of Schoenberg. Along with Alban Berg, he was one of the leaders of the new twelve-tone system of musical composition.

✐NDEX